Prayers & Wisdom
FROM GRANDMA'S HOUSE
Inspirational Warmth & Guidance
through Life's Journey

Alston Shropshire

Prayers & Wisdom from Grandma's House: Inspirational Warmth & Guidance through Life's Journey

Copyright © 2019 by K. Cannady

All rights reserved. This book or any portion thereof may not be reproduced or used in any manner whatsoever without the express written permission of the publisher except for the use of brief quotations in a book review.

Printed in the United States of America

First Printing
ISBN 978-1-943284-66-5 (pbk.)
ISBN 978-1-943284-67-2 (ebk)

A2Z Books Publishing Lithonia, GA 30058 www.A2ZBooksPublishing.net Manufactured in the United States of America A2Z Books Publishing has allowed this work to remain exactly as the author intended, verbatim.

CONTENTS

Message…What is God Saying? 1

The Introduction 3

Preface 5

Message… No one knows your devotion 8

Prayer…God is working behind the scenes 9

Message…Sorrow Worry Faith 11

Message… Don't Get Distracted 12

Getting Back to the Basics 13

Prayer … A prayer for all 20

When You Rise in the Morning 22

Ask Yourself… 31

Message… Everything attached to you 33

Reminder 34

Message… Think Back 35

Children 36

Message… Are you operating in these? 44

Hurricane Emily 45

Prayer… Prince of Peace 49

Hurricane Nate 50

Hurricane Patty 53

Hurricane Darkness	56
Prayer… Looking at myself	58
Message… Donations	60
Family is Forever	61
Reminder	64
Typhoon Tip	70
Reminder	73
Friends	74
Reminder	81
Hurricane Sandy	82
Work	85
Wildfire Luc	92
Scripture	94
Scripture	95
Money	96
Marriage	102
Hurricane Dorothy	111
Hurricane Heart	114
Scripture	118
Prayer… Petitioning Your help	119
Message… Piecing together	121
Reminder	123
Scripture	124
You can Make It …. Go to the Source	125

Hurricane Mattie Rose 130

Message… Time and Regret 132

Message…Unexpected 133

Summary.. 134

Message...What is God Saying?

What is God saying?

Are we having "church" with no change?

Are we having a "good shout," with no shift?

Are we judging a person for what we see and not looking at their story?

Do we know a few words and a few scriptures, or are we building a relationship with the Lord?

Are we delving deep into His Word until it completely fills us?

Are we continually pouring out, with no one pouring into us?

Whom are you mentoring in this Christian walk?

Who is mentoring you?

Is it a Jonadab or Jesus?

If God were answering these queries on your behalf, what would His reply be?

What is God saying?

Grandma

The Introduction

Sometimes, many individuals assume they have no one they can talk to or figure no one understands what they are enduring. People often expect judgment from the outside world or the people closest to them. When we get up to face another day, we may appear to others as having strength, having it figured out, or that everything in our lives is so splendid. In this text, you will find prayers, scriptures, a few songs, and words of encouragement for many trials you may face in life.

This text will allow you to recognize that everyone has their celebrations, storms, or crosses to bear. This text will give guidance and wisdom throughout Alston's life's journey. You will have a sense of joy, victory, strength, authority, power, favor, blessing, and endurance to get up and stand strong another day.

This text may allow you to consider. Hey, "if Alston can sustain those factors, drawing from prayers and wisdom from grandma's house, then maybe I too can make it." One key to praying that I've noticed is knowing that you are speaking to your best friend. Try taking the first step.

You can start by saying something as simple as this, Father, I thank You or Father, protect me; with time, you will get better. Grandmas' too, had her crosses to bear and roads to travel. How do you guess they came across such knowledge?

As you prepare to read, know you are entering the houses of two grandmas. Houses saturated with faith, a solid foundation, strength, class, wisdom, and endurance. These houses produced strong children and later generations. They knew that standing on the ROCK was crucial.

Enjoy reading the text and reflecting often. An earnest and pure heart can create change.

Preface

First, I praise God for instilling a purpose in my life before I was created. I praise God for trusting me to do His work by sharing the essential parts of my grandma's house, the prayers, wisdom, and His Word. I give special thanks to my spouse, children, parents, aunts and uncles, sisters, nieces, nephews, sincere friends, pastor, and first lady.

There comes a time in your life when you understand that what you have learned and sustained can encourage someone else. The storms and joyous events you have experienced can better serve the next person. Each storm is unique (as well as the conclusion). The way you approach it, face it, and walk through it can be the same. A smile, a great philosophy, prayers, self-encouragement, and things learned from a loving grandma about the love of Christ can change how you look at each experience.

You would think that after dealing with the unimaginable, like feeling abandoned as a child, dealing with physical abuse, molestation, and an unsuccessful rape, you have been through it all. As life will have it, there was more to encounter, including a divorce and the burial of a spouse. I have also dealt with failed relationships, untrustworthy friends, and life-altering illnesses while having a child with special needs. Often, life will have you thinking you are the only one in the world feeling the pain. Prayer would play a significant role in my life. Irrespective of the countless strife, this would always be the answer. A system that has proven to work.

I had to take the mask off and deal with the person in the mirror. Before I stepped into the church house, I walked into grandma's house. My grandmother's house was a place of familiarity, warmth, security, and yet a place that leads to the Lord's Word.

This text was painless to write, understanding that it developed from a place of sincerity and truth. I can declare it was natural to create, but the suffering was so unbearable through each storm; nothing was as difficult as those storms.

With all of today's technology and fast-paced life, I wanted to leave my sons something to get through life, through the dark days, as I know it will come to pass. Something that will one day drive them to pick up the Bible if they have not previously done so.

In the event they never did, I wish to leave behind a few scriptures and words of wisdom, the same as my grandma gave me. If they have called on the name "Jesus" from reading this text, I know they will recognize the name to call on in days to come.

 As you take the time to read this text, share it with someone else; your family, children, or someone in a storm.

I leave you with this saying that my grandmother often said to me as a child, "No matter what people do to you, always do the right thing because God sits high and looks low. He said vengeance is His."

My go-to scripture for many years has been **Psalm 57**, which talks about, *"the trap set by the enemy will be the trap they themselves will be caught in."*

As my grandma sits in heaven with a smile on her face, I know that writing this book has given her joy. Not the joy the Lord has given her, but joy, nevertheless. Momma, I know you are proud of this if nothing else.

Kiss to a Rose.

Message... No one knows your devotion

No one knows your walk and devotion like you.

Individuals may not welcome your walk as significant because they are so busy searching for your past.

You have to tell them they did not look back far enough. Those individuals must look way back to your foundation, the one you have in Christ.

Tell them to keep looking.

Grandma

Prayer...God is working behind the scenes

God is working behind the scenes on your behalf. Everything you have prayed for; He has heard you. Every single time you prayed in the name of His Son; God has heard you. Every tear you have cried, He has felt them. For every heartbreak and pain, God knows about them. Every care you have cast on Him, He will take care of them. God will rescue you. He will answer you. God will hold you. He will bring you through. God will make you victorious. He will make your enemies your footstool. God will heal your body. He will save your marriage. God will give you a husband/wife. He will free you from debt, and God will put food on the table. God will ensure the bills are paid. He will destroy the strongholds and soul ties. God will be there on the other end of things. His "will" shall be done in your life; YOU MUST believe that with everything in your soul. You can't make it without God. Father God, You said You would work it out for our good. You said that You "will" show us favor. You said that You "will" give us grace, mercy, and victory. We trust You. Intercede on our behalf in Jesus' name Amen.

Message…Sorrow Worry Faith

Sorrow looks back

Worry looks around

But

Faith looks Up

Message... Don't Get Distracted

Don't get distracted.

There may not be an anointing sound in my voice, but there is still praise in my message.

My packaging may not be what you expect, but there is still praise in my testimony.

My walk may not have always been straight, but the will of God has always ordered it.

GOD IS

GOD WILL

GOD HAS

GOD WILL CONTINUE

AMEN

Getting Back to the Basics

When going back to grandma's house, the basics, you must first start with please and thank you, followed by the proper yes/ no ma'am and sir. You must use excuse or pardon me and recognize when adults are in the room; the children are exiting. Never raise your voice and always respect your elders. Back to the basics, meaning that all children will go to Sunday school and regular church services. I remember walking around the corner to my mother's church for Sunday school and knowing I better behave, especially when mom is the Sunday school teacher and all. Back to the basics with Wednesday night Bible study and some Friday night revival services. Back to the basics of remembering your aunt being the church accountant/administrator. Back to the basics of uncles being on the deacon board. Now, where would that leave grandma, with the keys to the church, of course! She opened the church's doors every day for noonday prayer and for any other business the Pastor needed her to do. She did this until she could not attend services because she was in her late 90's and had glaucoma. The significant things learned at grandma's house at an early age were prayers and the Word of God. We had to say grace with each meal. You could not think of eating your food without blessing the food. Grace sounded like one of the following as a child:

God is great!
God is good!
Let us thank Him
For our food.
Amen.
God is great, and God is good,
And we thank God for our food;
By God's hand, we must be fed,
Give us, Lord, our daily bread.
Amen.

Come, Lord Jesus, be our guest
May this food by you be blessed.
Amen.

Both grandmas made these things standard. You could not close your eye to sleep with our saying our prayer. As a child, it sounded more like this:

Now I lay me down to sleep,

I pray the Lord my soul to keep.

If I die before I wake, I pray the Lord, my soul He takes

Amen.

This prayer was the only bedtime prayer I ever learned. You may know this one or have learned something different.

When it was time to learn scriptures in the Bible, the first one that grandma taught was one most children learned and had to memorize, for some church program or another, Psalm 23:

"The Lord is my shepherd; I shall not want.

He maketh me to lie down in green pastures: he leadeth me beside the still waters.

He restoreth my soul: he leadeth me in the paths of righteousness for his name's sake.

Yea, though I walk through the valley of the shadow of death, I will fear no evil: for thou art with me; thy rod and thy staff they comfort me.

Thou preparest a table before me in the presence of mine enemies: thou anointest my head with oil; my cup runneth over.

Surely goodness and mercy shall follow me all the days of my life: and I will dwell in the house of the Lord forever."

I never knew that staying at my grandma's house taught me the basic tools I would need for life in this scripture.

How old were you when you learned this scripture? I could not read or write, just repeating every word by memory verbatim.

This scripture talks about a shepherd watching over his sheep (a parent and a child). How He is leading them by still waters (did you know, you can see your reflection in still waters, even when there is chaos around you but in rushing waters, you cannot see yourself). You can walk through any storm or darkness and not be afraid because He is with you.

You can have a feast at a table with all of your heart's desire, right in front of the person or enemy that doesn't want you to have it. You are anointed from the crown of your head and have an overflow of oil pouring onto your feet. All of your days will be filled with goodness, mercy, and being in the safety of the Lord forever. These are the things that were instilled in my life. At the time, I was so unaware, just how much I would need them. I was being taught at grandma's house how to speak over myself with authority and power before spelling, writing, or reading.

When you go back to the basics of the things you were taught, you will realize that you have all the tools you need to make it with good teaching. Sometimes we forget those things because it seems like rules and restrictions at the time. As often told by my grandma, "know that in this life, you cannot lead (and have the respect) without first being able to follow. When I say follow, that doesn't mean with an attitude, or your lip poked out and constantly complaining — not giving it your all because you're not the one headlining." When she would give her words of wisdom, she would constantly ask, "Do you hear me?" and start over. I then learned to make sure I was listening the first time so that the conversation would be ten minutes instead of thirty minutes. Lord, what I wouldn't give to have a word of wisdom moment at grandma's house again.

Suppose we all could rewind the hands of time to listen to old stories, hymns, and saying our nightly prayer with grandma again. To hear my grandmother's stern but a soft voice with great encouragement would be a blessing. She was my biggest cheerleader. If she was here today, I could listen to a prayer going like this: "Come here and give me your hands and let momma pray for you."

Father God, we come to You today to pray over the life of Alston and all generations that come through Alston's bloodline. We plea the scripture Psalms 23 over them. We ask that You cover Alston in Your blood. Anything not of You make it flee. Destroy the demons and principalities coming against Alston's life. Heal, deliver, and strengthen Alston. Before Alston was born, she belonged to You. Bless Alston with an abundance of favor. Destroy all strongholds and generational curses waiting in the wing. We give You the Glory, the Honor, and the Praise; We know that Your yoke is easy, and Your burden is light. In Jesus' name, allow Your will be done. Amen.

To have that would be a blessing.

When you think back on your back to the basic moments, do you wish you had them again?

Did you take them for granted or enjoy every moment of them? If you took those moments for granted and wished you had them again, how are you moving forward to enjoy everything life has to offer? So you can savor every moment?

What back to the basic moments will you leave behind? How influential are you in the lives of others?

What are your favorite scriptures, your grandma's, or the person who made a difference in your life?

Would you say that your back to the basics is your core foundation of who you are deep down inside?

There is a saying that manners, respect, and morals will take you places money can't buy. But so will Jesus, my grandma would reply. And when you have Jesus, you will already have manners, respect, and morals. These core basic values will be something you will refer to more than once — the foundation of prayer.

If you have someone in your life that has taken the time to instill some basic core values into your life, hold tight to those words. No matter where you are in life, you will need rules, prayers, wisdom, and structure. Most importantly, in life, you will need Jesus.

A song comes to mind by Vicki Winans: As long as I Got King Jesus.

Prayer ... A prayer for all

Father God,

Thank You for waking me up this morning with a sound mind and a pure and sincere heart. Father, You are my everything, my all in all. No one is greater than You. I will forever praise Your name. Father, I ask in Jesus' name for You to sweep through my life, home, job, family, children, finances, and clean it to perfection as only You can. Cover and anoint it. Watch over it, Lord, ensuring no harm comes its way. Sweep through it, O Heavenly Father, leaving all evidence of Your presence. Father, allow all to see that Your face is over it. Father, pay special attention to my children. Lead and guide them throughout their lifetime, never letting go. Father, breathe on them, take away worry, frustration, stress, confusion, and the enemy's trick. Give them favor and mercy.

Touch everyone who took the time to read this prayer in its entirety. Grant them the desires of their hearts. Carry them through life, never leaving or forsaking them in Jesus' name. Amen.

When You Rise in the Morning

In the morning, most individuals dread the long laundry list of tasks they have to perform. They are playing out in their minds the lengthy and agonizing commute to a job they either embrace or detest. Wondering who will text or call for money today or wishing someone has overlooked that you were going to give them some money. They play out the meetings, court dates, appeal hearings, interviews for a nursery school, job, or college. Wondering what drama-filled story you will be listening to in the next few moments from that family member or best friend that has seemingly been going on for years. Errands of bills to pay, deadlines to meet, brunch/ lunch date, and doctor's appointments. Some may be fulfilling, and some may not, but when your eyes open, some days sound like this, "Lord, what do I have to do today or Lord, I don't feel like this." Sometimes it's just a deep sigh. Even if your day is something you have been looking forward to, like the closing on your first home, first day at the new job, cashing that check you have been waiting on for months, the day you sign the crucial deal you have been wanting, or getting that first car. None seems to have started with "Thank You Lord for waking me up and watching me through the night." —Not your first thoughts in most cases.

My grandmother often said you must be thankful for waking up in the morning. She would say sometimes, a morning prayer may save you throughout the day when you open your eyes, even if it's just to say, Thank You Lord, for waking me up. Morning prayers are how you should start your day. She would say that when your feet hit the floor, you should be praising God for what He is about to do and already has done. Look at it like this, she said, you didn't have to wake up this morning. He could have taken you in the midnight hour as you slept. There could have been a fire; a car could have crashed into the house. A tree could have fallen on the house. So many countless things could have happened while you were asleep. My grandmother would often say the things you ask should align with the word because the promises of God's Word will not come back null or void. Praying is something everyone should be in the habit of doing. Each day, you will become better and better at praying and giving thanks.

***(Isaiah 55:11 "So shall my word be that goeth forth out of my mouth: it shall not return unto me void, but it shall accomplish that which I please, and it shall prosper in the thing whereto I sent it.")

Let me share with you some scriptures from grandma's house about the morning.

Psalm 143:8 *"Let the morning bring me word of your unfailing love, for I have put my trust in you. Show me the way I should go, for to you I entrust my life."*

Psalm 90:14 *"Satisfy us in the morning with your loyal love! Then we will shout for joy and be happy all our days!"*

Psalm 5:3 *"In the morning, O LORD, hear my voice. In the morning, I lay my needs in front of you, and I wait."*

Psalm 119:147 *"I rise before dawn and cry for help; I have put my hope in your word."*

Let me share with you these morning prayers from grandma's house.

Father God,

We thank You for waking us up today. We thank You for guiding and protecting us along the way. We thank You for Your continued grace and mercy. We thank You for penetrating our hearts and mind. Father, thank You for the wisdom to recognize that we need You. We thank You for surrounding us with people who are of You. Father, we repent for our sins and disobedience; forgive us. In Jesus' name, Amen.

Father God,

I thank You on this day, for waking me up and for Your many blessings. As I look around in my life, I see so many grateful, humbled, and appreciative things. Father, no matter the storms that have come my way or maybe in, I know that You are with me. I know You will bring me to victory. I thank You for the blood that was shed that is still saving souls today. Father, Your presence is necessary for my life. Thank You for never leaving my side and being the ultimate parent, a child can have. Amen.

I come to You today, giving thanks and praising Your Holy Name.

I thank You for waking me up this morning and watching over me through the night.

I thank You for Your tender mercies.

I thank You, Father, for the trials and tribulations.

It's all according to Your Will and Plan.

I know that even in my valley, You will rescue me.

I know that when I'm on the mountain top, it's only because of You.

So, with all things, I will give thanks.

I thank You for Saving Me. For allowing me to have a relationship with You, that's always growing.

Increase my desire for You.

Increase my faithfulness.

Increase my love.

In Jesus' name, Amen.

My Father in Heaven,

I thank You for waking me up this morning and starting me on my way. Thank You Lord, because I know You didn't have to do it. Father God, thank You for the promises of perfect and unyielding favor You have on my life. Father, because You said it, I believe it. Father, because You said You would give me victory over my enemies, I believe it. Father, because You said You would put Your protective shield around me to keep me from harm and danger, I believe it. Father, because You said You're a healer, I believe it. You said You are a mind regulator; I believe it. Father, You said I would not beg for bread and that You are my provider, I believe it. Father, You said You would answer when I call on Your name; I believe it. In John 15:16, You said anything I ask of You; You will give it unto me; because You chose and appointed me to bear fruit. I believe it. Every morning that I rise, I will give You praise and glory.

In Jesus' name, Amen.

Deuteronomy 32:2

"My doctrine shall drop as the rain; my speech shall distill as the dew, as the small rain upon the tender herb, and as the showers upon the grass."

The song, Like the Dew in the Morning. (by Dr. Judith McAllister comes to mind)

Genesis 12:1-8

"The LORD had said to Abram, "Go from your country, your people and your father's household to the land I will show you. "I will make you into a great nation, and I will bless you; I will make your name great, and you will be a blessing. I will bless those who bless you, and whoever curses you I will curse; and all peoples on earth will be blessed through you. So Abram went, as the LORD had told him; and Lot went with him. Abram was seventy-five years old when he set out from Harran. He took his wife Sarai, his nephew Lot, all the possessions they had accumulated and the people they had acquired in Harran, and they set out for the land of Canaan, and they arrived there. Abram traveled through the land as far as the site of the great tree of Moreh at Shechem. At that time the Canaanites were in the land. The LORD appeared to Abram and said, "To your offspring, I will give this land." So, he built an altar there to the LORD, who had appeared to him. From there he went on toward the hills east of Bethel and pitched his tent, with Bethel on the west and Ai on the east. There he built an altar to the LORD and called on the name of the LORD.

Genesis 15:1-6

After this, the word of the LORD came to Abram in a vision: "Do not be afraid, Abram. I am your shield, your very great reward." But Abram said, "Sovereign LORD, what can you give me since I remain childless and the one who will inherit my estate is Eliezer of Damascus?" And Abram said, "You have given me no children; so a servant in my household will be my heir." Then the word of the LORD came to him: "This man will not be your heir, but a son who is your own flesh and blood will be your heir." He took him outside and said, "Look up at the sky and count the stars- if indeed you can count them." Then he said to him, "So shall your offspring be." Abram believed the LORD, and he credited it to him as righteousness. The song God Said it (by Patrick Riddick & D'vyne Worship /Cosmopolitan Church of Prayer comes to mind)

In grandma's house, you were generally given things to ponder. At that time, who knew they would reflect on doing the honorable thing, something from the bible.

One day my grandma told me, be thankful you have another day for fresh blessings and compassion.

Who knew that **Lamentations 3:22-23** specifies that, "Because of the LORD's great love we are not consumed, for his compassions never fail. They are new every morning; great is your faithfulness." Letting us know that we get to start fresh with His love and compassion each day. God is faithful.

She would repeat every morning, be thankful you have a roof over your head, food to eat, clothes on your back, and running fresh water. You are walking around this world, not recognizing that someone is praying for the very thing you are blessed to have. Alston, do you know you could have opened your eyes and been under a bridge, and do you know the person under the bridge is thankful for the bridge because they realize it was a chance their eyes might not have opened at all? The clothes you easily discard because they are not a popular brand or out of season, someone somewhere is overjoyed to have something on their body to protect them from the cold or something to switch into when wet from the rain.

She would tell me, Alston; there's someone with water dripping on their head from a roof leak, thankful they are being protected from the wind. A person in the wind is thankful they are not drowning in a flood. That same person that is in the flood is thankful they are not in their grave and still have the sense to call on the good Lord to give thanks.

I can hear her saying, "I can just thank Him all day long; you know you can't thank the Lord enough." She would say this with the biggest smile on her face as she walked away in her housecoat.

I would often sleep with my grandma, and as she would tuck me in, I became familiar with what she would say. "be thankful for this warm bed you are sleeping in, now and in the morning." We both would laugh, and she would give me the tightest hug and place the blankets on me.

My grandma's house felt like the biggest smile and the warmest hug always.

Ask Yourself...

When you sit back in the morning, are you taking a deep sigh and complaining, or are you thankful?

Are you enjoying your present home, or are you so fixated on a new home to where you are not making quality memories where you are?

Are you thankful for the car you have prayed for, or are you grumbling about every little thing, failing to remember when you were walking, carpooling, or on the bus?

Are you whining about tiny living quarters (your own place) and forgetting when you were sleeping on someone's couch?

Are you thankful for those noodles or not? Have you forgotton when your belly was rumbling?

Are you thankful for your morning dew? Are You thankful for your new supply of love and compassion?

Are you sincerely thankful for your first two blessings of each day, the ability to breathe, and your eyes opening?

How do you look at things in life, positive or negative, or just reality? Some individuals look at situations throughout their day as positive and negative. Some may look at it as reality, not seeking to decipher the good or bad. Finding a solution or how to make things happen, some may feel, is more important. Good versus evil (positive/ negative) has been around since the creation of time. Allow God to govern the evil or the negative elements and concentrate on the positive. Your storm can be your testimony, but so can your blessing. To God be the glory.

Message... Everything attached to you

Everything attached to you is blessed, covered, and anointed.

God will preserve you and this situation.

Get on your knees and pray.

He delivered me.

He can and will deliver you and your family.

Just keep trusting.

Grandma

Reminder

Don't give the devil more credit than God.

Message... Think Back

Think of all you have been through and magnify it for your parents. You are not the only one who carries a load. Often as children, we never see the endless sacrifices, tears, joys, suffering, and heartaches our parents go through. We continually concentrate on ourselves and our desires. But, if you count the trials and misfortunes life offers, look back on your parents and the crosses they had to bear. They, too, managed it all while making sure of your safety and wellbeing. After you have taken the time to look back, you just might look at them differently. Conceivably, with dignity, compassion, insight, and humility.

Father, no matter the hardship nor the triumph, we know we are safe in Your arms. No matter if it's sins or serving, You continuously maintained a ceaseless watch over us. We thank You Father, for all that You endured and sacrificed for Your children.

Amen.

Children

Proverbs 22:6 "Start children off on the way they should go, and even when they are old, they will not turn from it."

Deuteronomy 6:6-7 "These commandments that I give you today are to be on your hearts. ⁷Impress them on your children. Talk about them when you sit at home and when you walk along the road, when you lie down and when you get up."

Isaiah 54:13 "All your children will be taught by the LORD, and great will be their peace."

Exodus 20:12 "Honor your father and your mother, so that you may live long in the land the LORD your God is giving you."

Proverbs 13:24 *"Whoever spares the rod hates their children, but the one who loves their children is careful to discipline them."*

1 Corinthians 13:11 *"When I was a child, I talked like a child, I thought like a child, I reasoned like a child. When I became a man, I put the ways of childhood behind me."*

There will invariably be two views that may have a unique perspective. The view of the child and the view of the parent. All of which may suggest they are correct in their point of view. Before I can indeed delve into anything from grandma's house, I must express this.

As a child, I preferred to read, and I loved to talk. I was strong-willed, determined, spoiled, independent, arrogant, and incredibly intelligent. I had to run the show, and I had to have the last word. You could not tell me anything, and I settle for it. My mouth often got me into trouble. I was not reluctant to stand up for myself.

As a child, you were expected to remain in a child's place and not talk back. You were not told things you felt you should have known. This was just how things were then. I was dealt some cards that would send that sarcasm, and determination into overdrive. I was a handful. Looking at it now, I do not know how I did not end up in jail. I don't know how they did not give up on me, either, not saying a good deal of them may not have. Not having an older sibling, I had to fend for myself and made sure I could back up everything I said.

There was no one to talk to who would understand the devastation of the things that were happening in my life, my storms. Just as each hurricane has a name, even children have storms they have to deal with, many of which may be unknown to the adults. When you start to feel defeated on the inside with no outlet, here comes bullying, withdrawal, and rebellion. As a child you are trying to find your way through this. You are trying to process it all, with little or no experience.

You have children growing up in foster care at birth or left to be raised by other family members; once they become knowable of what's going on, they begin to think of "why did my parents leave me?" You have children struggling to figure out why their friends has more clothes and shoes than them. Why am I not able to hang out with the cool crowd? Why is my mom constantly working and not home with me to help with homework? How am I supposed to retain the information the teacher gave during the morning to be able to do all of this work alone. You have some children being bullied and don't know why. This is too much for a child to process, when some children can't tie their shoes at this age.

So, what does a child want to do, hurry up and become an adult? Just so they don't have to follow any rules, do any homework, and just come and go as they please. Children think they have it hard, and in their own right they do. Why, because they're entering a part of life that's new. Children have their own challenges that they face every day as well. You are going to bump your head a few times. You are going to slip up more times than not. Don't get me wrong; some get it right; some listen to every word from their parents and do not stray. Well, I on the other hand, butted my head more than a few times, I just don't think I was feeling the impact of the hit the first time. I hit my head so many times, I probably thought it was a dance or something. I slipped, skidded and ran headfirst into so many things in life; I know the knees of the people praying for me was bone to altar. I am so sure that they ran out of oil.

Jesus probably had to come down the stairways of heaven to refill everyone. Jesus was probably trying to give them more words to say in the prayer because I just know they ran out. Not where I was going to jail or anything like that, I never stole or was into drugs, but it was always something. We often like to say its puberty, but really, we need to get to the issue of what is going on. Being rebellious is a cry for help, but a help from what? Each child has something different going on.

In grandma's house, I did not talk much about what I was dealing with. I felt like she was older and probably would not understand. I just held it all in. I mainly acted out.

Children are misunderstood a lot of the time as well. In my situation I was spoiled, and I knew it. I lacked respect for certain situations. I was in a storm and did not know it (what kid is really saying, let's meet at recess to talk, I'm going through a storm) let alone know how to discern and deal with it.

On the other hand, you are the parent of a child or children, thinking to yourself, these children have no clue. I assumed I was going to be grown, have fun, do what I want, when I want, and with whom I wish. When you develop into an adult, you have more rules to follow than you did as a child. You have the rules of a job, the school or the daycare your children attend, the rules of the marriage, and the rules of being a parent. You have bills, bills, and more bills. You hardly get adequate sleep at night; you are somewhere right now praying for a nap. If you are a parent, you must remember what goes around comes around, thank God none of my children act like I did, not even through adolescence. I must admit, I have excellent children. The rod that my parents spared me; I did not spare my children.

As a parent, you are trying your best not to make the same mistakes you feel (not to say this is always true) your parents made with you. So here you are deciding on whether or not to be the cool parent and trying to understand why your parents carried out the decisions they made. So, you chose not to be the cool parent and lay down the rules. In the midst of all of this, you are having your storms. See, the storms don't stop. There's a season for everything. And hurricane season is now in full effect. One storm after another, the job, children, marriage, bills, and your health is just under attack. So now your children are staring at you in the same eyes that you stared at your parents and now you are looking at your parents from a sympathetic view.

Full Circle

We as parents, don't (in most cases) give our issues or concerns to our children. We realize that we are here to support and maintain in the best way we know-how. How can they possibly console you and give you the answers on how to bury a spouse? They are not married and most evident they are children. Heck, you cannot process and comprehend it yourself. How can they advise you on what went on in your childhood, they weren't there? They may be dealing with their issue, and what you are revealing is foreign to them. This will be due to lack of experience. Truth be known, no parent would want their children to face those difficulties.

As the child has their full circle, which will be when they become a parent. The parent too will have their full-circle moment, as they have children. The realization comes later on while you are in another phase in your life. We all need to consider that in life everybody has their crosses to bear even children. We all need to be prepared and equipped for the things that this life brings. No, we may not face all the same storms but a storm we will face. Learn to pray, don't just listen to the prayers of grandma's house, embody them, because the wisdom being passed on is to encourage you. The source she is trying to lead you to, is there to help, protect and give you strength. If you didn't call on the name Jesus as a child, even in a breakfast prayer, you most unquestionably would call on His name at some point in life.

Romans 14:11 "As surely as I live,' says the Lord, 'every knee will bow before me; every tongue will acknowledge God."

I am so thankful that as a child, my family thought enough of me to lay down a foundation. One that was in the Lord. I want everyone to know it is never too late to get it.

At grandma's house, there was consistent prayers, largely for me, I expect. There will come a day when you have to pray for yourself. So, when I became an adult, I knew what to do when times became troublesome. Pray. I knew what to do when I had to encourage someone else. Pray with them. That is the type of wisdom that came from those houses. When I have to encourage them, I let it be known, with all things, look to God. He is your source. In life, prayer, scriptures and talking to God will be your must have.

***When you are about to blow your top in frustration, with being a parent or being a child, just tell God- thank you. Thank you for the position, to learn and teach. Thankful for trusting that you can complete the task; with all things prayer is the answer.

We are all God's children, and we must know, within all of our heart, that He has our best interest. We must trust and believe that He knows the way. We must realize that we are safe in His arms, not in rare times, situations, or moments in life, but in all. This is not for a selected group of people; it is for us all, at all times.

This makes me think of the song Safe in His Arms (by REV. Milton Brunson\Pamela Crawford version)

Message... Are you operating in these?

Are you operating in these?

Koah (Great ability).

Exousia (Great in authority).

Dunamis (Great in Miracles).

Kratos (Great in reigning).

Hurricane Emily

This is the one storm I stood in battle. The buck stopped with me when it came to my father. I was special — the only child. Then entered a wife. The nerve of him, I felt. No one asked me. I'm yet a kid, but my opinion mattered. Heck, I was essentially a grown-up, in my mind anyhow. My father always spoke about how much he adored my mother, so that was all I knew, and here she was, breaking up this family (this is true testament of when a child needs to stay in a child's place). You are correct when you assume no adults have had a conversation with me. I mistreated her for not being my mother, and she mistreated me because she wanted my father to herself and wanted children of her own with him (this is what I believed at the time). This was a different type of storm; this storm was slow-moving — way more rain than anything else. I loved to play in the rain, so that's what I did. She was more like a sneaky cat; she got a kick out of causing a stressful environment when no one was looking. She would not mistreat me in front of him, but when he wasn't around, she would. Being more like a big, bold lion, I never ran away from an opportunity to stand in my boldness and usually responded as lightning and thunder in the sky, always loving when an audience was near because I always knew to come with facts, and I did.

As misguided as I was, I was never corrected, well occasionally, but not enough. I was grown for my age, and I would be very contemptuous to her and her family. When she was rude and cunning, so was I. The things I said, were as if I was a forty- five-year-old, who smoked Virginia Slim, and hung at the local bar on Friday and Saturday nights (I definitely should have been chastised). I was young, but I could talk trash. I got this from watching the older adults in the neighborhood. At an early age, I could distinguish if someone were playing sides, being fake, or just plain ole didn't care for me— she was one.

I can say that she taught me a thing or two about her position (stepmother) that would come in handy later in life. I gave her a run for her money as well. The feeling was mutual; we did not care for each other. The actual storm didn't come until one day, my grandmother's phone rang, and it was my father. They talked for a while and then I was called to the phone. This call rocked me to the core. I recall it like it was yesterday. Hey, we are expecting a baby, with such excitement. All the resentment came out that day about everything. It came out of nowhere. Things that I had been holding in for years.

I said everything I ever felt — no holding back. I let him have it. I regret it to this day, not what I said, but the way I said it. It hurt, and it cut deep. But it was the truth, and everyone knew I never lied. I cried and prayed so hard that day. The prayer I prayed; I don't know if I would take it back. We got another phone call about a month later; they ended up having a miscarriage. My father would later die at the age of 42. I never made it right with my father. This would be my biggest regret today. I did reach out to her to apologize for not staying in a child's place. She still is the same and has done other things after my father's passing, but I did the right thing and apologized for the part I played. I didn't understand the dynamics of the relationship of my parents (their divorce), but he had every right to move on if it was going nowhere. Years later, my mother would explain her side. This would explain so much.

You should never want someone to lose their child. You should never be disrespectful to adults; it's wrong. A child should never intertwine in adult affairs. You have no clue of what the story is, nor should it matter. Stay in your place, honor your mother and father, so your days may be long (this is in the bible, so His Word does not come back null or void). Is there karma in a storm? Are your days being shortened due to not honoring your mother and father? It does make you wonder.

Everything you think is a storm, maybe just a little rain, or maybe it's just life. If something did not work out in one place, you must move on. Why sit waiting on a train that's never coming back. Time waits for no one. Live your life. In saying that, communication is key with all parties involved.

Grandma often said, don't stir the pot. It can get messy if you don't know what you are doing.

You have to realize YOU ARE NOT ALWAYS RIGHT, just as you own when you are right, own when you are wrong, and fix it. The apology I gave would come years later, way after my father's death. I apologized for not staying in a child's place and being disrespectful to an adult, not for what I said, I don't' think.

Prayer... Prince of Peace

Father God, the Prince of Peace, I ask that You still the waters of the raging seas. I ask that peace be still on today. Calm all the noise of today, so that I can hear Your voice. Remove the things of the past that do not have a place in my future. Remove the things that are wreaking havoc in my mind, home, and life. Father, help me stay focused. Give me the desires of my hearts, while exposing those things that mean no good. Whatever is using me, and manipulating me destroy it in Jesus' name, Amen.

Hurricane Nate

Here is another story about a childhood hurricane; as I said, children also have storms. Children love to have fun with friends, especially at school. Whether a child is on the playground, at recess, or horsing around in the classroom. Children have storms. You have children dealing with whom to hang with, what cool things to wear, grades, and trying their best not to get bullied. Whether your parents got you the latest clothes from the town you lived in or got your clothes from another area (up north); still, it had to be hot. As the holiday vacation ends, it is time to go back to school. Walking to school, especially after a Christmas holiday, you are prancing in your best gear. I would be no different. My first day back, I wore my sheep's wool coat that my mom purchased from up north, with my Calvin Klein jeans, a pair of Etienne Aigner sneakers, and Izod shirt.

I thought I had arrived— I couldn't wait to wear it. However, soon as I stepped on the playground, there was the heckler, appreciating that my outfit was hot; I didn't sweat it. The next thing I knew I was shoved into the, and my outfit was ruined. Everyone was laughing. Devastated and with a hole in my heart. I had to get up. The entire front of my clothes was covered in mud.

How would I ever live this down in schoolyard history? Everyone saw it. Life's not fair, I cried to my grandmother, it's just not fair, and why is this happening to me? How can I go back there? They are going to laugh at me all over again. My grandmother said, "This is nothing but a little dirt; this can get cleaned. The kids will be laughing at the new thing soon, don't worry about what people think. They laughed and mocked Jesus; you think they won't do you the same? Come here, give me a hug (after I was cleaned). It's going to be just fine, guess what I have, some more new clothes." She pulled out this beautiful green velvet blazer with Calvin Klein jeans. I was grinning from ear to ear. She escorted me back to school and said, "I'm going to cook you something good for when you get home, and that coat will be looking brand new. I'm going to fix it. You just be good in school. What happened today stopped nothing from moving forward; this was just a minor misfortune. Alston, setbacks will happen in life too; it's just a setup to move you forward and give God "a good praise."

To this day, I don't like bullies, and I don't like to see others mistreated in any way. It gave me a complex about being the underdog.

Once I forgot about being in the mud, I realized grandma made everything "all right." I also got to see the other surprise outfit my mom had for me.

Tell God, thank You for the storm. Realize, they talked about Jesus, and He still moved forward in His purpose.

Hurricane Patty

Here is a story about a childhood hurricane; again, children have storms too. Bright and vibrant with a good future ahead. I was always in the school spelling bees and a good girl. I always made good grades, and a B+ was the lowest. This would be the first storm. This would change me from a shy but smart girl into someone else. My living arrangements weren't normal like the rest of my friends at the time; I just knew something was off. I stayed with grandma during the week and my mom on the weekends. This was normal living for me, especially after my parents' divorce. One day, while playing in the house, passing licks with my cousin, I would soon stand face to face with my storm. That last lick must have hurt pretty badly as the tears began to flow from my cousin's face. I was laughing as if the victory had been won. Finally, I had won;

this was the title belt, so to speak. Not recognizing in those tears, there was a storm brewing. This storm would be life changing. My cousin said, "That's why your mother is never coming back." I was shocked, and there was a dead silence.

You could hear a rat pissing on cotton. Now everyone is crying. That's not true; take it back. That's not true, take it back, or I'm going to hit you again. As the table turned, and the cousin is now laughing. Grandma, Grandma, say it's not true, my momma is coming back. This time there were no words of wisdom, no come here and give me a hug, just listen, your mom went to find a better job and a better environment for you; she will be back to get you. I didn't want you to leave me. Whether the reason was true, the way of finding out left a hole in my heart for many years to come. The lick I passed surely wasn't as painful as this.

Once the storm's initial impact was over, grandma made everything all right. My grandmother always helped me see the brighter side of things. My grandmother did not want me to be uprooted so fast. I was her favorite, so it was hard for her to let me go. As children, we don't understand the sacrifices parents make. It did give me a better opportunity in the end. My mom got that great job and provided a better environment. I was able to fit in fashionably and was no longer bullied in school. I went to a diverse school (multi-cultural and ethnicities). It was a better school. It changed my life forever, for the better.

As children, we don't understand the sacrifices parents make. We don't understand how hard it was for them to leave us as well, but back then and even now, hard decisions are a part of life.

God does everything for the greater good. It truly was a blessing in my case. Parents have tough choices to make every day, and while some may say that was or was not a good decision. Teaching and seasoning had to come from grandma's house.

HIS WILL... HIS WAY

Thank you, Lord, for the teaching and seasoning.

Hurricane Darkness

Some hurricanes in life you don't know are coming. Some storms have not necessarily resulted from a decision you made. They can be a result of the things that are around you. Some of these storms are so horrific, traumatizing, and damaging that you can barely deal with them. Those storms, sometimes, are just between you and God. There may be things that trigger a memory of this storm, but hold tight to your faith and thank God that you are not in that dark place anymore. You may have more than one of these types of storms. Most people don't stress bout these storms. Not saying it did not devastate you, but you have chosen to let it go or just pushed it deep down inside. The "boogie man" is very real, and so are horror stories. Everyone has a "hurricane darkness".

Giving a storm to God is a marvelous thing. It is the absolute best thing one can do.

Prayer... Looking at myself

Father God,

I come to You today, giving thanks and praising Your name.

Father today, I'm ready to look at myself. I am ready for You to clean the mirror to see better.

Too often, it's easy for me to focus and examine other people's flaws and circumstances.

What they should or shouldn't do? How they should or shouldn't do things?

I have yet, or not as often examined myself. What could I do better? What should I have done? Help me, Father, to see and acknowledge those things within myself that need to be changed.

Father, fix those areas in my life. I need to step out of the way of judgment because only You can judge. I need to start seeking, living, and sharing Your Word. Work on me, Heavenly Father, and remove all things, not of You. Make the mirror clear so that I can see that it's not always someone else. It could be me, my flaws, and my issues. Search Me. I desire a better me, and there is no other way than through You.

In Jesus' name, I pray.

Amen.

Message…Donations

What are you donating to your surroundings and the people in it? God gives us peace, joy, understanding, compassion, empathy, happiness, loyalty, favor, grace, mercy, friendship, sincerity, love, and countless other positive things. Can you donate or give those things to the people who surround you? Let's donate a little kindness today. Let's donate a little compassion. We don't know or need to know what's going on with someone to do it. Do it because it's the right thing to do. Do it because that's what we would want. Give some time to God. He is most deserving. If you don't have a church home, visit one with someone close to you.

Family is Forever

In life, we all come from someplace, whether good or dangerous. This is the one fact from birth we had no choice. Everyone's point of view of their family is their own. You have individuals with excellent reminders of their family or home life. Then you have individuals with unbelievable stories of theirs. One thing that is undeniable, no matter if you move far away, disassociate, or disown them, there is something about the blood that is forever. It is embedded in the DNA to whom you belong. As you get older, you become wise enough to know that everyone's family was doing the best they knew how in both instances. A child, in most instances, is given the best that the parent has to offer with the accessible means.

Does this make you less of a family because you have issues that are often complicated to work through? No! Just because your issue is that a parent left due to whatever storm they were facing but placed you in the care of a family member doesn't mean Billie Jo down the street isn't dealing with some form of issue in their two-parent home. You have been raised by someone more fitting to take care of you at that time. There could be an abuse of many things going on in Billie Jo's home. Both homes have issues; both houses will always be family and are doing the best they can to work through their storm. If you haven't noticed, no one was born with a manual; you may have been born with another sibling, but no book. Every family member's breaks in life will not be the same. You have a purpose that God has for you. Do not look at life as not being fair because you are not driving that BMW 745, and your brother is. You may or may not have a Jaguar Pace in your future. You must always be thankful for what you have. You may have some family members needing more help than others, and some may be more blessed, and that's ok. Family is a key part of life. You should never be in competition with the family, and you should never let anyone fall. You should be able to help family and strangers alike, IF you can.

If we look deep inside, I'm confident we can uncover some upsetting actions that have transpired at the hands of the family. Some things may have cut really deep. When you glance at the bible, it instructs us to forgive and to love those that hurt us. People tend to forgive their friends, coworkers, neighbors, and church family but will not for their own blood. When you look around at funerals, 95% is going to be your family. Ones you have and have not spoken. Ones that you may still be upset. The party crew you used to hang with may or may not be there; the ones you confide in may not be there as well. But uncle Howard, the same one you didn't want to take to dialysis, or aunt Sally, whom you could not take to the grocery store, will be in attendance. The friends you gave the most to might not be there. The cousin or sister you often belittled because he/she was not as established as you; will be there. They might have been the ones who often asked to borrow money and couldn't pay it back who are in attendance. They are going to be the ones your children can rely on in the days and years after your passing, in most cases.

Luke 6:32 "If you love those who love you, what credit is that to you? Even sinners *love those* who love them."

Matthew 6:14-15 *"For if you forgive other people when they sin against you, your heavenly Father will also forgive you. ^{15}But if you do not forgive others their sins, your Father will not forgive your sins."*

Mark 11:25 *"And when you stand praying, if you hold anything against anyone, forgive them, so that your Father in heaven may forgive you your sins."*

Matthew 18:21-22 *"Then Peter came to Jesus and asked, "LORD, how many times shall I forgive my brother or sister who sins against me? Up to seven times?" ^{22}Jesus answered, "I tell you, not seven times, but seventy-seven times."*

Reminder

"Humble yourselves, therefore, under God's mighty hand, that he may lift you up in due time."
1 Peter 5:6

Both grandma's houses were big on family, faith, work ethic, love, and the family name. Something about the name of whom you belonged to meant something. Being a part of a family of prominence, you were recognized, observed, and had to carry out careful steps in life. I recall at both houses being told charity starts at home. The outside world may forget you, but the family will not.

When I was a child, there were reflections of cleaning the house, cooking food, and traveling to work. I have a lot of military family members (including my sons), and everyone was always staying busy doing something constructive. As those grandmas' would say, an idle mind is the devil's workshop. As I reflected on major holidays, I would think about the smell of savory food and the joy of laughter overflowing. Those were the moments that made grandma the happiest. To see the children, fly in from all parts of the world, grandchildren playing, and everybody ready to eat that home cooking. If there were any family conflicts, they were customarily set to the side. There were rarely any, however.

In some families, there is much judgment on one thing/ person or another. We all must remember this particular saying I was taught; no family or person is perfect. The only perfect one is God.

Luke 18:19 *"And Jesus said to him, "Why do you call Me good? No one is good except God alone."*

Mark 10:18 *"And Jesus said to him, "Why do you call Me good? No one is good except God alone."*

She would say, "Alston, your mind is on so many things. This family, my family, will be just fine, because I have given you all to the Lord. I go to church every day and pray for my family and the generations that will come from my bloodline. My mother has prayed (my great grandmother passed away at 102 while living with us) and her mother has prayed for the generations to come. So, you stay focused, pray for your family and remember to always say, for me and my house we will serve the Lord. Always walk in forgiveness. Sometimes the prayers that are answered may not have been one that you prayed for yourself. It may have been that of your ancestor. When you may have possibly strayed from the Lord and His teaching, it may have been someone standing in the gap for you."

Joshua 24:15 *"But if serving the LORD seems undesirable to you, then choose for yourselves this day whom you will serve, whether the gods your ancestors served beyond the Euphrates, or the gods of the Amorites, in whose land you are living. But as for me and my household, we will serve the LORD."*

For the Rest of My Life (I'll Serve Him) by Rev. Timothy Wright

I had a remarkably close and unbreakable bond with my grandmother. Some people may have had the same. Some may not have known their grandparents or just may not have shared a tight bond. Think about what type of grandparent you would like to be, what memories and words of wisdom you would like to leave behind if your grandchild would think to write a book about you. What type of legacy would you want to leave, and would it be pleasing to you as you sit at the gates of heaven? Would it be pleasing to God?

You see, I now missed the days I often grumbled about. We would gather eggs from chickens and pick vegetables, *berries*, and snap green beans. My grandmother made marvelous preserves. My favorite was apricot. We would walk to pay bills, stop by the seafood guy to get fresh shrimp. I had great memories with them. They thought I was their personal hairdresser whenever I was around.

The bible she would use still sits on the chest of drawers today in the family house. The bible has my writing in it that I made as a child. I can hear my grandmother saying, "Don't mark in my bible." I remember visiting various churches with her. Riding on the church bus to small towns, seeing many preachers that are sure long gone, but the word they instilled lives on. I remember washing and hanging up clothes with her. I remember whenever there was a family member in need, they came to grandma's house with heads hung low or sadness on their face, but when they left, they would leave with a huge smile on their face and happiness in their heart. Maybe because of the words of encouragement she would give, it could be the scripture she would often quote; some may think it was the newly received money in their pockets. Nevertheless, they didn't leave the way they came. Looking after the family was key. She would often say that if no one ever reached down to pick you up, you would still be lying there when you didn't think you could get up. So many people think that it's someone else's job to help. People other than the ones that share the same bloodline. Yes, some family members may make it difficult or think that money grows on a tree, but if God is continuously making way for you to provide for both of you, then why not? You are only able to do what you can, and if you can't, don't. But if you can do it, thank God for allowing you to be able and continue to pray for one day soon; they won't need your help because they will be able to do it on their own. Grandma said the people who often sow seeds have had seed sown into them. Some sow due to not having anyone sow into them at all. This has consistently stuck with me. I have sown unto many. I have also been sown upon.

Typhoon Tip

Hurricanes, typhoons, and cyclones are essentially the same, a tropical storm. The origination is what establishes the distinction. There literally was a typhoon name tip. According to [AccuWeather](), Tip occurred on October 12, 2012. It was classified as Earth's strongest and most massive storm in history. This is the storm you assume is going to kill you; that is until you get to your next storm. Before this storm came, the sun was shining, and life appeared to be good. When you pray for things to be revealed, you must be aware of what will creep out of the darkness. When you pray for things, it can come in the form of a storm. That is one thing I no longer pray. I now say, protect me and keep me covered.

I pray to the Lord to convict anyone who wants to do anything that will bring harm to me, and they change their minds.

The things I endured in life up to this point would make you think I have been through it all until you see Tip coming. Tip is the storm that I felt the pain on all sides. This would have me look at who I am, question my self-worth, and what is in me that's drawing these types of energies—from the beginning, feeling like I should have evacuated when the warning came and was advised to leave. I decide to wait it out. This storm will leave your wig/ toupee hanging on by one strand. Multiple infidelities throughout the marriage will have you yanking on to the third cord.

During this storm, there will be children created outside of the marriage. Imagine finding out an increased number of children you knew nothing about. I found out about secrets so dark they fall under hurricane darkness in this season. These are things that I would ultimately have to take to my grave. Violation, public humiliation, and everything in between is the storm of the lifetime, so you think. The devil is standing there, just laughing, thinking I was out. I did too. How do you not think you can get back up after multiple blows, jabs, uppercuts, and body shots? It felt like I was in the ring with a boxer. Two strands of hair left, eyes barely opened, and down on my knees, but God has my back. I know grandma is in heaven, praying, and saying come here, give me a hug. The mere thought of her voice makes me get up.

God is building your Faith for something much stronger than this.

The faith the size of a mustard seed, grandma said, that's all the Lord need.
Matthew 17:20 says, "So Jesus said to them, "Because of your unbelief; for assuredly, I say to you, if you have faith as a mustard seed, you will say to this mountain, 'Move from here to there,' and it will move; and nothing will be impossible for you."

Reminder

Speak to your storm.
Peace be still.

Friends

In grandma's house, there was not an assemblage of friends there. She was quiet and was all about family. I constantly wished to have friends over to spend the night or just to play with. To do the things children do, travel to the park, skating ring, or the movies. She would repeatedly tell me; you better be mindful of needing so many friends and learn to be by yourself sometimes. I used to assume this was so mean. I preferred to be a free spirit.

A social butterfly, so to speak, I recall a conversation between my grandmother and me, and she said, "You are so concerned about hanging around a crowd of friends, receiving and experiencing them, you don't even know who you are." Of course, I responded, I know who I am; I am Alston. You will recognize that the sole friend you need is Jesus if you realize that. Jesus is the ultimate friend. There is no time He will not respond. Jesus will never let you down. Jesus never talks about you, and He holds your secrets. When the going gets tough, Jesus doesn't scatter or leave you behind. Yes, a friend can cause you great happiness, but only Jesus can bring you joy. You state that you know who you are. But tell me, who are you? Where will you be in the next five or twenty years? Do you or your worldly friends know that? Heck, your mom doesn't either. Baby, I don't even know.

I bet you Jesus knows. Yes, the things that you hold way deep down inside, Jesus knows that as well. When you take the time to have Jesus as your friend and establish a steady and genuine relationship with Him first, you will be able to distinguish who your real earthly friend is. When you learn to appreciate a true friend in Jesus, you will not settle for anything less. She would go over the song lyrics (but singing slightly off-key), What a Friend We Have in Jesus (the version by Mahalia Jackson)

What a friend we have in Jesus
All our sins and griefs to bear
And what a privilege to carry
Everything to God in prayer

Oh, what peace we often forfeit
Oh, what needless pain we bear
All because we do not carry
Everything to God in prayer

Have we trials and temptations?

Is there trouble anywhere?

We should never be discouraged

Take it to the Lord in prayer

Can we find a friend so faithful

Who will all our sorrows share?

Jesus knows our every weakness

Take it to the Lord in prayer

John 15:10-15 *"If you keep my commandments, you will abide in my love, just as I have kept my Father's commandments and abide in his love. [11]These things I have spoken to you, that my joy may be in you, and that your joy may be full. [12]"This is my commandment, that you love one another as I have loved you. Greater love has no one than this that someone lay down his life for his friends. [14]You are my friends if you do what I command you. [15]No longer do I call you servants, for the servant does not know what his master is doing; but I have called you friends, for all that I have heard from my Father I have made known to you. "*

What friend have you experienced like that? I am a kid, so I have no inkling of what she is speaking about as she is preparing her famous homemade biscuits, using the teacup to cut it out in the perfect form. As I was regularly in the kitchen observing all of my grandmother's cooking, I just craved to go outside and play, however. Those regular kitchen conversations and observations would fine-tune my cooking abilities. Just not with those biscuits.

Who knew this was one conversation that I will reflect on years later and the questions I should have asked?

As a child, friendships are often innocent, with maybe a few spats here and there. Your friends aren't there for any circumstances or hospital stays. During this time, it is mainly family. You have not had any relationships with the opposite sex to confide in with your friends. Again, being too young, you are unable just to pick up and leave and see your friends at will. You are at the age where it is just Tonka trucks, Barbie dolls, and the latest outside game of the day. Nothing major has happened. You have yet to be in a position to question friendships or motives. Fast forward to a first-time relationship, school dynamics, the change in the home, three-way phone calls, and adolescence; friendships have evolved quite a bit. Fast forward to adulthood. You learn during hard times that a relationship, loss of a job or family member, illness, a business, incarceration, success/money, a family addition, marriage, and divorce who your real friends are. This is a perfect storm in itself if you are walking through life with a person you believe to be a friend, but they are not. The reason why I call this the perfect storm is because you are in the middle of a storm already (loss of a job, illness, or divorce), and now you are colliding the storm of a friend who is going to spread your business, are jealous, possibly being a Jonadab and giving bad advice. A friend that can constantly be on the receiving end until you have no more to give. A friend that is never willing to give to you.

Sure, we can also have those friends that may seemingly be in a storm longer than you think they should be (judgment), but always remember you do not know what is ahead of you, so don't be so easily angered or frustrated. Your storm may just be around the corner, and this same person may remember you being so kind to them during their storm- holding the umbrella.

We all have so many friendship stories; some are great, some long-lasting, and others that have just been one big lesson. However, when you talk about the friendship, you finally discover with the Lord, whether from your back to the basics or you're building that friendship today, that friendship is the ULTIMATE blessing.

Let's think about something.

When you lost that job, a way was made for something better. Whether it was the pay, a shorter commute, fewer responsibilities, more time with the family, a larger office, a better benefits package, weekends off, or you met your spouse at the new job and going on ten years together. There was a better outcome on the other side. What a great friend is Jesus?

When that illness came, as devastated as you were, Jesus was there. You may have been heartbroken over losing your longtime friends. It may have been a scary feeling as you were going through this life-altering illness; however, He surrounded you with some friends that literally wiped the tears away. What a great friend is Jesus? He knew what you needed.

Jesus is a friend that knew what you needed when you didn't have a clue. When you buried that spouse, He cleared the path and protected you underneath His wings. Such a mighty shield, at such a young age, you didn't understand until later. What a friend to have? Jesus.

This message isn't about bashing a friend but more like grandma said in that house while making those biscuits. "When you take the time to have Jesus as your friend and build a solid and sincere relationship with Him first, you will be able to discern who your real earthly friend is." I started praying like this during the lonely days.

Father God, I thank You for being my ultimate friend, a friend in my time of need, joy, and sorrow.

A friend who will be there in the beginning, middle, and end.

Father, surround me with earthly friends whom You have anointed and appointed to my life.

Allow our path to be a two-way street without envy, jealousy, or strife.

Father, allow us both to recognize that You have sent us to be a part of each other lives.

Allow us to cherish, respect, love, and have compassion for the friendship.

In Jesus' name cover it in your blood.

Amen.

***I** want to shine on the fact that God should be your first friend. It will set the tone on how you choose relationships. It would have saved me a lot of trouble. The friends that I thought would be at my first husband's funeral were not. When you have all the drama in the marriage, you have your cheerleaders. But when that marriage leads to divorce, you find yourself standing there all alone. When you are in the hospital fighting for your life on numerous occasions, it was not the friends that I was talking to every day that were there. It was not the everyday friends who would feed and check on my son. So, as I am moving forward and reflecting on things. I could have done many things differently — choices that I made and things that I accepted. Pointing the fingers is very easy, but you have to take accountability for the actions and choices you make. I am no different. Taking conversations seriously as children and the willingness to listen will help you later on in life.*

I should have asked her more questions about the meaning of a real friend. So now, my ultimate friend is God. He sets the example of what type of friend I will accept and what type I desire to be. Everything starts with you. I had to unmask and look at myself. We all think we are the perfect friend. We all may be looking at our friends with judging eyes. We must understand, no one owes us anything. We also must understand that we should be what we require from others.

Reminder

Go to the altar.
Take it to the Lord in prayer.
Most importantly, leave it there.

Hurricane Sandy

While young and thinking life is full of fun and games, periodically, you may get a storm to give you a reality check. Well, storms come to teach you a lesson or bring you a blessing; occasionally, it's a little of both. Sometimes you have to get your priorities together. Especially when you decide to have a child at a young age, as a young adult, you have to learn which road you want to take quickly because some roads are dead-end or may lead to destruction. One day, my friend and I decided to take all of the children out for a routine walk.

The weather was nice, and the children (our sons and our little sisters) were tired of being cooped up in the house. Even though we were young adults, we had acquired separate living quarters. We certainly thought we had arrived. During this walk, my friend saw someone she recognized, and they exchanged words. To this day, I don't remember what their issues were. I just know she said they had words early when I was not there. The next thing I knew, a gun was out, and more words were exchanged. As things died down, we continued with our walk. The story of who the guy was and what was going on made up our conversation throughout the rest of the walk. The whole time I was thinking my mom is going to kill me if something happens to my sisters. Let me finish this walk and call my mom to pick up my sisters and son. My friend told her family what was going on, and now everyone is looking for everyone. Again, I would be there in the middle of it all. While hanging out later that night for a little fun, we walked home as it was getting late. Walking in the middle of the street as we could see our place in the distance, here pulls up this car, the same person from earlier. Hey, I've been looking for you; as the conversation went on, I interrupted them. I just have a question; why would you pull out a gun while children are around?

I would understand on that day that when two individuals are talking, you mind your business, especially if it has nothing to do with you. The look on his face let me know he was talking to my friend and that since I wanted to be a part of the conversation, I was welcomed right on in. He went to the trunk of the car and pulled out a double-barrel shotgun and put it to my temple. My little short life, flashed before me; all I could see was my son's cute face and the building to where we lived. Thinking I should hit him with a bottle, common sense let me know the gun will surely go off then (thank God for common sense). As my friend was crying and begging for my life, please don't shoot was all I could hear, but all I was thinking was, "Lord if you get me out of this, I'm going to sit down and get my house in order. I have a son to live for." My life was spared that night. We walked home; this would be the first time I picked up the bible and plea Psalm 57 over my life. I could not imagine my son living without me. After hearing the guy's girlfriend saying he should have killed y'all and the children (this was not even my issue, but I put myself in it when I asked that question). I was so upset that someone could feel so heartless. Needless to say, exactly two weeks later, he was killed by another female.

I had to call on the source to spare my life, but I learned a valuable lesson, keep your mouth closed sometimes. You don't have to address everything. I should have been quiet and praying. I should have stayed at my mother's that night as well. That could have been my last night. That night could have been the night that my mother buried her child. BUT GOD.

Sometimes the storm we have is self-created. I had to let that sink in.

This storm would lead to psalm 57 being my go-to scripture moving forward.

Work

Grandma often referenced everything to the bible. So, what does the bible say about work?

Genesis 2:15 *"The LORD God took the man and put him in the Garden of Eden to work it and take care of it."*

Colossians 3:23 *"Whatever you do, work at it with all your heart, as working for the LORD, not for human masters,"*

Psalm 90:17 *"May the favor of the LORD our God rest on us; establish the work of our hands for us- yes, establish the work of our hands."*

2 Thessalonians 3:10 *"For even when we were with you, we gave you this rule: "The one who is unwilling to work shall not eat."*

Genesis 2:3 *"Then God blessed the seventh day and made it holy, because on it he rested from all the work of creating that he had done."*

Proverbs 21:25 *"The craving of a sluggard will be the death of him, because his hands refuse to work."*

Well, the one generally referred to in grandma's house was "II Thessalonians 3:10," more often than not, if you don't work, you don't eat, was all I could grasp at such a young age. It would be safe to say the work ethic of everyone that came out of those doors was remarkable. It was instilled at an early age, and everyone had to pull their weight, be it having chores, assisting with the grocery bags, even as a child, you had to do something. Counting the number of tasks completed by noon made you feel lazy if you only had one task done. You could not just throw anything together because it represented you. "Didn't God put you together nicely?" Yes, grandma, well, your work should reflect that. You must do things as if God is examining the work. "Do you want God to see sloppy work, half done anything coming from His child? Well, make sure you do it right the first time and with a pleasant attitude."

Those were the earlier days of lessons learned and instilled. If you were to think about work today, some might feel overwhelming excitement—others, well, let's just say, they may not be that excited—irrespective of if you have obtained your dream job and have the best coworkers surrounding you. You have a lot to be thankful for. You may have the best supervisors and managers there is to have. You can also be working for the best company. A company that matches dollar for dollar on 401k benefits. You may have the best health insurance, a top-dollar salary, and the company car. To top it all with a cherry, you may get recognized every week for a job well done. The company may purchase lunch for the entire office, pay for a company trip, or provide little perks like an updated phone or tablet. If you are really at a great company, they may even send out birthday cards for your children. Even with great work ethics and accomplishing so many tasks a day, you may get one or a few of the things listed above, but not all. But still, you must be grateful and humbled, even if you are quite deserving.

Now, if you fall on the side of dreading work, not having the best supervisor, manager, benefits packages, and your pay barely covers all the things you need, you must still be thankful. You still should have the best work ethic and attitude. Why do you say? Well, 2 Thessalonians 3: 10, *"the one who is unwilling to work shall not eat,"* and Colossian 3:23, *whatever you do, work at it with all your heart, as working for the LORD, not for human masters.* I cannot forget to mention, Proverbs 21:25, *the craving of a sluggard will be the death of him, because his hands refuse to work.* Oh, the life lessons of grandma's house.

When learning about work and work ethics at grandma's house— I am going to tell you the things you did not learn —You did not learn through these conversations about the multi-personalities of a workplace, the easily agitated supervisor, the micro-managing manager, or about the coworker who steals everyone's food. You were unaware that the one job title you applied for held several other job descriptions. You were not aware that while holding your title, you are completing the work for others while falling behind on your work (without recognition or a pay increase). Later on, you would come to learn the constant complaining every morning that millions of us do before heading into work. If I had a penny for everyone who does this, I would be wealthy. There is a long running saying and feeling of the majority, "Overworked and underpaid." At grandma's house, you were not aware that once your regular 9 to 5 ends, the other job begins, family, children, church duties, a second job, and the marriage. You just saw everyone coming in and going back to work.

The lesson I learned out of what grandma's house was not about the coworkers, the supervisor, the pay, or how well it took care of the bills you had. What she said was, complete the work right the first time with a pleasant attitude. Your work is a representation of you. You must do things as if God is examining the work. No matter the subject, the focus was always on God. At the end of the day, God is your source, even your source of strength, to get the job done. He is the provider. With good work ethics and a pleasant attitude, maybe a visiting company sees your name on everything (all of these extra job descriptions you are completing) and makes you a dream offer. Maybe, the quality of work you are putting in is making the VP notice that the Director of Operation's work is not of quality or their own merit and promotes you to that position. Maybe the person stealing the food, come to find out they are sleeping in their car or just have been evicted (not saying this is right, because they may not know you are in a similar storm but chose a different route and not steal).

So, whether you are in your dream job, an overworked position, or still searching for a job, still be thankful for the position you are in. Do your job as if God is watching, continue climbing up the ladder and even if you are on the basement level of your job, know that God visits there too. God can be protecting you from a job that appears to be the best but is draining. So, try not to be discouraged and look at things positively.

You must not stress or take everything so personal in working at any job. Focus on the job and give it the best that you can. Pray every day that you walk into the building; you have a stress-free day. Ask God to show you in the areas or places you need to be seen and hide you beneath

His wings when trouble is near. Most people have a work prayer at their desk or a bible on the desk. I had my Psalm 57 just in case and read it every morning before I clocked in.

(To the chief Musician, Altaschith, Michtam of David, when he fled from Saul in the cave.) Be merciful unto me, O God, be merciful unto me: for my soul trusteth in thee: yea, in the shadow of thy wings will I make my refuge, until these calamities be over past.

I will cry unto God most high; unto God that performeth all things for me.

He shall send from heaven and save me from the reproach of him that would swallow me up. Selah. God shall send forth his mercy and his truth.

My soul is among lions: and I lie even among them that are set on fire, even the sons of men, whose teeth are spears and arrows, and their tongue a sharp sword.

"Be thou exalted, O God, above the heavens; let thy glory be above all the earth.

They have prepared a net for my steps; my soul is bowed down: they have digged a pit before me, into the midst whereof they are fallen themselves. *Selah.*

My heart is fixed, O God, my heart is fixed: I will sing and give praise.

Awake up, my glory; awake, psaltery and harp: I myself *will awake early.*

I will praise thee, O Lord, among the people: I will sing unto thee among the nations.

For thy mercy is great unto the heavens, and thy truth unto the clouds.

Be thou exalted, O God, above the heavens: let *thy glory* be *above all the earth."*

Now, of course, working a 9 to 5 is the most natural thing to think of when it comes to the word work. There are other forms that I gained knowledge of as well in grandma's house, working in the church. Working in the church might as easily have been a 9 to 5 because she labored so regularly there. My grandmother was dedicated to opening the church's doors and aiding the pastor and first lady in whatever manner she could. She stayed blessed and highly favored in the eyes of the Lord, I felt. I doubtlessly ever heard any grievances about any work she undertook, at the church or the job. Working in the church brought about so much joy. She would say, "How can you not be overjoyed in doing the work of the Lord?" Seeing such pleasure in this form of work, no wonder why so many of the family members have been an extension of the church in one way or another.

I recall being taken to Fox music store downtown. We went there to purchase my first tambourine. She said I know you are young, but you too can do the work of the Lord. The original one I got was plastic, blue and white. She said you could send praises up to the Lord by beating on your tambourine in church. After being so efficient, she promoted me to an adult tambourine, a wooden one. You could not tell me I wasn't carrying out the work of the Lord. I was out beating some elders in the church. From doing the work of the Lord with a tambourine in hand, I moved up to the children's choir, then the young adult choir. The family's absolute rule was, do not play in church and do not play with God. I still, to this day, go by that.

With my own church home, I still believe in doing work in the church as if God is watching my work. Having some huge shoes to follow, I only can pray I measure up.

We all know we have to walk in our own shoes with our signature footprints, but in some way, we all are looking at a pair of shoes, trying to fill those while making our mark in this life's journey.

(Empathy... Compassion...Walk in it ...*Boldly*)

Ask yourself this…

Am I faking it until I make it? Will that work with God?

What type of work am I putting into the church?

Am I sincerely working in the church, or am I working in the church with the same blah attitude I have on my regular job?

Whether you answer any of these questions through this book honestly or not, I will never know; however, God surely does.

Wildfire Luc

Some people get fascinated with hurricanes, such as storm chasers. Always remember the disclaimer, put your safety first; these are critical conditions that fluctuate within the blink of an eye. You are putting your life in danger and your family at the risk of losing you. A storm will leave a hole in your heart, but occasionally there will be one that just leaves a fear, just like a parent instructing a child not to touch the fire on the stove, warning that it will burn. A wildfire is distinctive from a hurricane; they burn. When burned from this storm, you will not go back. There will be something in your gut that when you see flames, it will remind you of how hot fire can really be. These can come in the form of relationships, marriage, jobs, family, or friends. Now, whether it be going to church or hearing it in prayer, you will often hear the saying of the Lord protecting you in the midnight hour.

In grandma's house, she would say that when you wake up, you need to thank the Lord for keeping watch over you while you sleep. You must understand, the enemy never sleeps. Satan has his workers working around the clock. They are never ceasing on how to turn your life upside down. These types of wildfires will give you a revelation on praying without ceasing. This storm came in the midnight hour, as everyone was sleeping in a hail of bullets. This wildfire wanted death.

Peacefully sleeping, no one was aware until morning. There was evidence of shell casings, bullet holes everywhere, and shot-out windshields on the car. Every night I say my prayer, and every morning, I tell God thank you because I know I did not have to wake up. Can you imagine your kids burying their mother at a very young age? Every inch of my house is anointed with oil. The entire grounds have been walked and prayed over. The water to put out the fire came from the Lord above. You must be careful out there, you cannot afford not to have a relationship with God, and you don't know what is awaiting you in the midnight hour. I can hear grandma say, not today, devil, not today. After experiencing a wildfire, when you see one standing in front of you, your gut will send fear through your body to warn you that danger is near. Your gut will let you know this is not the setting or people for you.

Scripture

"But He said to them, why are you so fearful? How is it that you have no faith?"
Mark 4:40

Scripture

"I sought the Lord, and He heard me, And delivered me from all my fears."
Psalm 34:4

Money

1 Timothy 6:10 *"For the love of money is a root of all kinds of evil. Some people, eager for money, have wandered from the faith and pierced themselves with many griefs."*

Hebrews 13:5 *"keep your life free from love of money, and be content with what you have, for he has said, "I will never leave you nor forsake you."*

Matthew 6:24 *"No one can serve two masters, for either he will hate the one and love the other, or he will be devoted to the one and despise the other. You cannot serve God and money."*

Luke 6:38 *"Give, and it will be given to you. Good measure, pressed down, shaken together, running over, will be put into your lap. For with the measure, you use it will be measured back to you."*

Proverbs 27:23 *"know well the condition of your flocks and give attention to your herds."*

As a child, you have no value for money; you just learned it buys you the things you need. You surely didn't understand how hard it was to come by. You would always get money to place in Sunday school and the church pan on Sunday mornings. You might not have received any for the store (to get chips, candy, or McDonald's), but you sure got some on Sunday for church.

Money does make the world go around, but I was repeatedly told that if you don't have a dime in your pockets, you should have food, a roof over your head, and the bills paid. This information mainly came from both houses. Neither wasted money as there were always the things imperative to make the house run available on hand.

Once my grandfather passed away, nothing ever fell short because all the children learned how to fix something or had great jobs in order to have the improvements completed in grandma's house. So, my grandmother never needed or worried about anything. I understood that quantity did not mean it was the best in those houses, but the quality did. My grandfather taught me that. You might as well buy the best quality, so you don't have a bunch of broken junk lying around, plus it will last. Pay the money in the beginning, and you won't have to pay double in the end. A multitude of backtracking is a misuse of time, and time is money. He would also say, money is not worth the paper it's printed on, so don't get caught up with money. It will come and go. Try being a good person with good character and be well respected. Let God provide for you. He was an Army veteran, worked a legitimate job, and saved. I saw him give a lot of money away, and I don't know if he was rich or not, but he always gave. My other grandfather was a little different with money. You had to work to earn his money, and once you earned it, then and only then would he give it. He owned a few businesses and worked hard for everything he had. Both taught me the value of a dollar and about work ethics. They told me not to be out here begging for money, and as God blessed others with it, God can bless me too.

In life, there will always be bills; you will always need a place to stay, food to eat, and transportation to get to and from, so you must be prepared. Money causes the most stress. How will I come up with the money for the rent this month? You may have lost your job or tried to obtain your first job. Prayer and faith are always needed when money is involved. Money has caused friendships to end, strains in the marriage, and frustration on jobs, if you are not getting enough. So many people think that money can buy you happiness, but it can't, it can only buy you things and when the money runs out, then what?

My grandmother would say that just because someone has money does not mean you are entitled to it. It doesn't matter whose money it is, your parents, friends, or family. You have to make sure you have your own. Chiming in, one of my uncles, "yea, God blesses the child that has their own," I did not find out this was from a blues song that Diana Ross sang until later in life. They had me thinking this was from the bible. It still would be a very true statement, which I would need to remember.

The family always pushed stability and tithing. I never understood it as a child, I just put money in the pan, but as I got older, I knew what I was supposed to give. After many storms in my life had passed, I remember a conversation about tithing. I was told, no matter what you have to do, you set aside your tithes first, and you will not have to worry;

everything else will fall into place. I have been doing this, and I have not missed a meal, nor have I had anything turned off, and all of my bills have been paid (this is a true blessing).

Sometimes I did not have a clue of where the money was going to come from. I never liked asking for money from others, only my family, and that's if it was a dire need. So, going back to grandma's house, back to the basics of putting something in the pan, that Luke 6:38 held true. This is not the only time in my life this has held true. I recall going to church, and I did not have any money to put in the "pan" as my grandmother called it, nothing but two pennies. I cupped my hand and put it in there, not wanting anyone to see. I went home, and there was my cousin with $150.00. I was so overjoyed with tears; I could not believe it. I went and purchased some groceries with my new blessing. Well, after expressing what had happened, to my mom, she replied, "you never read the story in the bible, Mark 12:40-44 about the widow?" I had not, but I made sure to read the passage as I, too, had lost my spouse recently.

Mark 12:40-44 *"They devour widows' houses and for a show make lengthy prayers. These men will be punished most severely." [41]Jesus sat down opposite the place where the offerings were put and watched the crowd putting their money into the temple treasury. Many rich people threw in large amounts. [42]But a poor widow came and put in two very small copper coins, worth only a few cents. [43]Calling his disciples to him, Jesus said, "Truly I tell you; this poor widow has put more into the treasury than all the others. [44]They all gave out of their wealth; but she, out of her poverty, put in everything-all she had to live on."*

The words from grandma's house holds true when she told me, God knows your heart and your needs, and that He would take care of you. It moved me to tears again. After talking to my mom, I went to my grandma's house to tell her what transpired and about the story in the bible. Not that I was telling her anything new, she read her bible continuously every day.

"Look at my Alston," she said, as she smiled as I walked up the steps. I told her the story, and she was so pleased, not about the money, but that I had learned a story in the bible. She said you will remember this story for the rest of your life. Alston, always go to your source, and He will provide. You have a Father that's rich. "My dad is rich, I said?" Your Father in heaven, He sure is. He has a paradise waiting for you, but you always must do the right thing, and this earthly money is no good there; you can take nothing of this world when you finally go to Him. That would not be our last conversation, but this one, too, let me know that I will forever be ok, as long as I do the right thing and continue to go to the source.

I had not too long moved back to the town, and I assumed that moving back home after the death of a spouse and other storms would be a good idea. I did not know that God made all these things happen so I could be closer to home because soon, she would be going home to be with Him.

Ask yourself...

Do I trust God to provide all of my needs? Then why worry?

Do I believe that I will be the victor in this financial situation? Then why worry?

Do I believe He will work it all out in the end? They why worry?

Do you believe hard work pays off? Then why worry?

Marriage

Ecclesiastes 4:12 "though one may be overpowered by another, two can withstand him. And a threefold cord is not quickly broken."

When engaging in a conversation about marriage, the newbies get a twinkle in their eyes and butterflies in their tummies. Not to say the long-timed married couples do not as well; it's just a marginally different twinkle—a twinkle with wisdom and experience. A twinkle of we made it. After weathering the challenges that came our way, we are nevertheless in love. Our family is still intact, and we love each other more. Couples should always understand that every marriage is different. You have some newly married couples that were married previously and kind of know the ropes. They also know that marriages come with different storms and different seasons. One minute you are vacationing in St. Lucia, and the next, you could very well be looking for separate living quarters. You have other married couples where this is their first time at it and are both walking with fresh eyes. They are full of hope and love.

<u>Genesis 2:20-24</u> *"so the man gave names to all the livestock, the birds in the sky and all the wild animals. But for Adam no suitable helper was found. So, the LORD God caused the man to fall into a deep sleep; and while he was sleeping, he took one of the man's ribs and then closed up the place with flesh. Then the LORD God made a woman from the rib he had taken out of the man, and he brought her to the man. The man said, "This is now bone of my bones and flesh of my flesh; she shall be called 'woman,' for she was taken out of man." That is why a man leaves his father and mother and is united to his wife, and they become one flesh."*

Mark 10:9 *"Therefore what God has joined together, let no one separate."*

Marriage is not for the faint or the weary. Both must daily put in effort, love, prayer, and effectively communicate with one another. When I am speaking of communication, I do not mean talking at someone. I also do not mean talking without listening and without comprehension. I have learned that the M in marriage stands for the Master because you must make certain you have the Master in your marriage. The symbol of the threefold cord, if you look at the picture, it looks a bit weathered; there is some unraveling there. Yet it is still tied together firmly, interwoven with each other. Understand that if anyone falters from the strand, it will weaken the hold. By this, I mean losing the husband, the wife, or God.

No marriage will be storm-free. The length, type, and harshness of the storm may vary. Some people's experiences will be the same. Some may have storms early on, and some later on. There is no way to be fully prepared for a storm. You are so busy with life and marital bliss; you don't necessarily see it coming or think it will ever happen to you. Some may see the writing on the wall and either choose to ignore it or not think it would have a direct hit. I'm not talking about a few raindrops. I am not speaking of small disagreements like paying the bill next month versus now, or the logic of investing in a minivan over a sports car. These nevertheless can have a big blowout, not devastating in most cases. In its own right, these minor disagreements are something that should be taken seriously.

A huge hole will surely come with physical and psychological abuse. I am speaking about a hole that cuts out the foundation of your soul, like infidelity, outside children, secret lives, drug habits, public humiliation, and finding out about children previous to the relationship. I am talking about a controlling person that came out of nowhere, like a light switch; as soon as you said, I do.

We likewise cannot forget emotional abuse. These things tend to have you lose yourself and also are not gender specific. Some people are in marriages where there is sexual abuse. I am talking about a real hole in the heart. The strands are becoming frayed. We are talking about a storm of total violation, betrayal, lack of trust, respect, and perhaps love. Imagine a spouse bringing another person into your home, in your bed. Do you see the devastation in that?

A place of comfort for you and your family. A place where you have long memories together. The place where your children were born and raised. Now, do you get the picture? What part of life prepares you for this type of valley (*Yea, though I walk through the valley of the shadow of death, Psalm 23*)? What did your mother, father, even grandma's house teach you to prepare for this? For any of it as a matter of fact. Most people do not discuss their marital issues. Back in the days, concerns were swept under the rug, a vast hush; no one spoke about these things. It may lead one to wonder how equipped are you?

You must understand that emotions nor reactions are always the same. Everyone handles things differently. Let's look at this, you are married, and you are feeling the betrayal of a spouse because they have spent the shared savings on either drugs, a fly-by-night Ponzi scheme, or that extra-marital affair. Your level of trust and respect may be gone. You feel violated. You may leave. You may have another person that is more forgiving and able to move past it *(I will fear no evil: for thou art with me; thy rod and thy staff they comfort me, Psalm 23)*. Again, marriage is not for the faint, and you do not know what you will face. Your intentions and promises are to face them together as you stand at the altar, some of you with your family, friends, and God present.

I have never heard any disagreements, seen, or heard of any infidelity in the marriages of both houses. Does this mean they have never faced any obstacle? No! What I saw was constant prayer and love being shown. As I think about it, I've never seen a head hung low, heard a raised voice, or seen a tear shed. This would not be the type of home I would share in my marriage. The time my storm came, grandma was gone to her heavenly home. I would often mentally speak to her and say, "Why is this happening to me? Life just isn't fair." I just sat there with a hole in my heart. I felt the warmth of grandma and as tears rolled down my face, and my eyes began to swell. I could imagine her saying, *come here, hug me, you know tears are prayers too.* Even though it was like a frog in my throat, and I could not speak. God felt every tear and answered them all.

All marriages are not this way. You can have a few rainstorms, arguing about food, family things of that nature, and everything else is pure joy. You can be that awesome couple with all the great functions at your house with family and other married couples, going on couple's trips and playing couple's games. You can be going strong for 50 years. For that, to God be the glory.

I Won't COMPLAIN

The song I WON'T COMPLAIN by REV. PAUL JONES comes to mind

No matter the type of marriage you have, go to the source. Easily said, some might reply, but God can and will restore it. God doesn't put any more on you than you can bear. Even the devil must get permission before he can attack. Why would God grant this? Because God will be with you the entire time, He knows how strong you are. God wants you to walk in your authority. He wants you to lean on Him. God doesn't want you to forget; God is that third strand in the marriage. You should start praising God when trouble comes because you know He will meet you on the other side. Always remember by His Will and His Way. I am not saying that you want a hole in your heart; I surely didn't. I had my faith tested and tried, but I still had the victory, and without an obscure doubt, I know He is a healer. The hole in my heart is filled with joy. With the space I'm living in now, I'm so happy. So, the tears God is seeing are those of joy. Trouble doesn't last always. Always look up to the hills to where your help cometh in a marriage.

***When getting married, always remember that no one is perfect. Two imperfect people with different personalities, ways, opinions, and beliefs join into a union, so there will have to be compromise.

Another part of marriage is often not spoken of, no not divorce, but being a widow/ widower. Sometimes people say it's a part of life, and for the most part, it is. One day, one of you will leave this world before the other; each individual is hopeful that it's in their later years of living. For the most part, it is, but a percentage of this happens in younger years, some a few days after being married. I have heard where it has happened hours after the ceremony. No matter the time frame, it is one of the most painful things a spouse will have to deal with. No matter the length of the marriage. No matter the countless arguments or storms. No matter how joyous the union was. This is one experience that is not thought completely through. It does not matter if it's during the marriage or before marriage. It is usually something that just happens. Even in purchasing life insurance policies, it is not with the intent that this will soon happen. No one thinks about the death do you part in the vows as a possibility. Once you are married, your partner is your life; as in the order of the Bible, everything and everyone is second outside of God.

You have spent so much time, had countless conversations with them, and had so many memories, hopefully, more sunshine than rain. So, when something like a death takes place, it leaves an enormous hole in your heart.

Most often than not, once the funeral is over, there is no one there to help pick up the pieces. Once the last slice of lemon cake is eaten, and all the chicken is gone, and that's a lot of chicken; It's just you or you and the children. It is back to life as usual for everyone else. Remember, this is your storm. There may not be anyone to buy the children some clothes or make Christmas the same as it was before. No one to go over the bills with, to keep you warm at night, take care of you while you are sick, or wipe the tears from your eyes. No one to help you deal with the pain that's so deep inside you feel it in your soul. Again, this is your storm. The house you once had that was so full of family, friends, and fun times; it's gone. How do you deal with it at any age or stage in the marriage?

Well, each person is different. But the pain is so seemingly the same. The loss is familiar, no matter the nature. A year later, where is everyone, two, three, or ten years, if not for you, for the children? Remember, children have storms too. This is a storm a child didn't know was coming either. It is hard to make it in life with your parents (so a child thinks). Can you imagine not having one or both to a tragedy or illness? Can you imagine trying to be there for your child when you are a shell of yourself? Can you imagine watching your spouse leave this world in your arms and still not knowing they are leaving? You don't necessarily know that there are support groups. The people around you living with their spouse may know about them; chances are they don't either. Tensions and emotions are rising high due to the weight of this type of storm. Depression may set in, and you may not even know it. Life is going on around you, and no one else notices either. Not one person has mentally put themselves in those shoes. How could they, they haven't experienced it? You must realize that this is something that you will only understand when you are standing in the storm.

In this storm, you don't know it is going to turn into a mega-storm. You have other factors intertwining into one. A factor of where is the life insurance—there is none. You started the process, got a quote, and were supposed to deposit the money, but a shoe sale came. You're young, so you don't' know that 250,000 quotes would double. How will you come up with the money to pay for a funeral? A factor of people thinking you had something to do with it, for a policy—a policy you don't have. Heartaches and lessons are in this storm.

No matter the storm, grandma's house taught me to be bold, stand strong, know that you are the child of the Most -High God, and you can and will make it. Do you remember what grandma said about mud? It's just a little dirt, but it cleans off. Grandma also told me a scripture that

I would need for the rest of my life. John 15:16 says, "*You did not choose me, but I chose you and appointed you so that you might go and bear fruit— fruit that will last— and so that whatever you ask in my name, the Father will give you."*

All I say now is, Jesus, help me through this.

I am always thankful for the storms of the past; it made me better prepared to face things in life. Whether being married or losing a spouse, those storms made me stronger and wiser. I am now standing on that solid foundation grandma's house stood on, the Rock. I am showing my children how to stand and stand strong. Through it all, the rod and the staff will comfort you.

No matter if the water that surround you is raging. Stand firm on the rock.

Hurricane Dorothy

Young adults have storms too. As a young adult, you feel like you are on top of the world. But who knew a young adult's storm would mirror an older adult?

This day would start with sunshine and doing ordinary things that anyone would normally do with their family. The normal tidying of the house in the morning, even though tired from the emergency room visit with one of the children the night before. At the same time, planning an evening dinner with family, nothing like a couple's night out. No one would be prepared for the magnitude of the storm ahead. Nothing and no one prepared you for this type of heart-shattering, wiping your world off the map type of storm. You have your nine-year-old son come into the house saying someone is fighting down the street. You go to the door to see what's going on. You see nothing. Then, as you walk up the street to get to the park (assuming this is the only place it could be), you pass a man standing on the step to one of the houses; you think to yourself, dang, he must have been in the fight, as he is undoubtedly beaten up. But, the more you walk pass, you see your spouse lying on the floor of a house as if to be knocked out. Being a young adult, you call the family to say your spouse had been knocked out, evidently from a fight. They are on the way. You head back to the house, but before you get there, a lady is saying, is that your spouse, I'm so sorry, and you're like the family is on the way; what are you sorry about?

Nothing is clicking in your head. You are just angry and trying to find out what is going on. Then she begins crying and pleading with you about how sorry she is. As you approach the house and walk in, you see the dazed look in their eye, just like a boxer. You are telling them to get up; the family is on the way. You keep saying get up, get up, get up, and they are not getting up. You continue yelling, get up. Now you are being pulled by officers to escort you out of the home. They need to take you to the station. You do not understand why you have to go to the station over a fight. Nothing is clicking.

We need you to go to homicide. Still, nothing clicks. You are being questioned on the events of the day. Again, nothing is clicking. You are now asking where your spouse is. Seeing that clearly nothing is clicking and you are not used to being in this type of situation and that the word homicide is not registering, you are now taken somewhere else, a place that will never leave your memory—the medical examiner's office, a picture that will forever remain stained in your mind. You are now identifying your spouse, looking at pictures of them laying on that table

— a deeper hole than you can ever imagine. You are rocked to the core. How can you ever tell three children this? Who can you talk to about this? What twenty-something-year-old person is going through this? Who at this age is planning a funeral, picking out a casket?

The one and only time you have the nerve to question God.

You look around; you see nothing, no future, no smile, no sunshine, not even rain — just darkness.

You are allowed time to sit in the wilderness; even Jesus went into the wilderness. He, too, came out.

But you cannot allow yourself to get swallowed up into the black hole. Jesus, please shine a light on me. If I fall, my children will fall. I cannot let them fall.

My mother and aunt (foundations of grandma's house) said, you don't have time to waddle; you have to keep it moving. You have to live for these boys. They are watching you. They need to see strength. They need to see you not give up. Those words they gave me motivated me to fight, live, and stand strong.

I laid down, but I didn't die too. I got back up. Five months later, I will be diagnosed with a life-altering illness (congestive heart failure, lupus, and arthritis).

Hurricane Heart

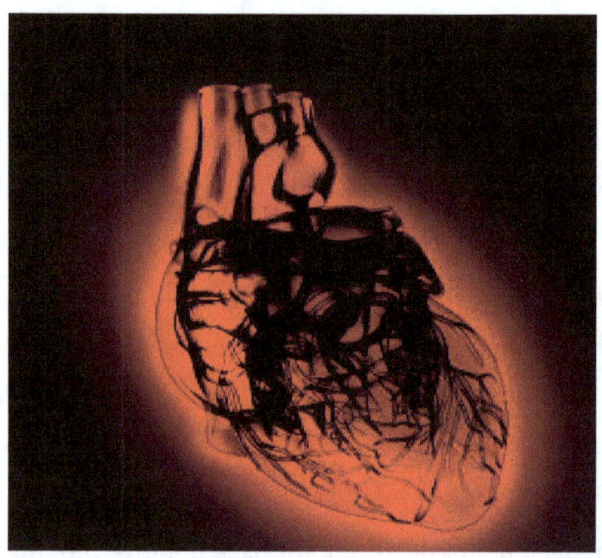

Not only is a storm devastating, but it also leaves a hole in your heart. Illness is another storm that you don't know when it is going to hit. The only thing you are thinking is how long it will last. This is the type of storm that really tests your faith. No one can pay to make this storm go away. You cannot divorce this storm; this is not the bully on the school playground that you can call the teacher on. Five months after dealing with the last storm, this storm hits, lasting over 15 years. While going through other storms, I am seemingly getting weaker.

One day I went to the emergency room due to not feeling well. That was when I entered my new storm. The doctor walked in and said your heart is functioning at 15 % (ejection fraction), and you cannot leave the hospital. I fell back, shy of hitting the floor, thinking to myself, my phone doesn't last long on that much time, I have to come up with a plan and have a family meeting with my children. I need to sell my other property to get some things taken care of in the current home. I had to think quickly. Surgery, the doctors would shortly say after, you need a pacemaker. I completely blanked out; you must be kidding me. Until we can get you onto the calendar, you must wear this durable device. I just want to go straight to my grandmother's house and crawl in her bed, but she is no longer here. I am in a place where there is no family. I thought about it and realized I have a church family. I called my pastor and first lady; they were the closest human beings to Jesus I knew. I'm just getting back into the church good; I've been attending two-and-a-half years, I think. I can't imagine the weight pastor carries because I just dumped it on them as if they were my mother, father, auntie, and grandmother all rolled into one. Knowing there was nothing physically they could do, but I felt I needed an extra amount of prayers to the man upstairs.

That Sunday, I knew I needed to go to the source. I laid it on the altar. I broke down and cried as if no one was there. The entire church prayed for me and checked on me. It kept my spirits up, as my faith was surely tested.

After the surgery, I would be tested again. The pacemaker got infected, and when that happens, most people die. I was fully septic, but for some reason, it did not go in the wiring into the heart, which would have killed me. I was released from the hospital with the understanding that home health would be there in the morning for treatment. That process was not set up correctly, so I reached out to a few sources. I had to pay someone to assist me with administering my infusion treatment, not before collapsing in their arms. After a short time, I was able to get into a facility. The initial treatment was not strong enough, so they gave me the strongest medication they had. Initially, I was receiving treatment hours on hours a day, seven days a week, then every day for a few hours for the next few months.

My heart percentage went up to a little over 30% (ejection fraction) for a while, and the ole hurricane whirled back around; my heart stopped, but the defibrillator shocked me back to life. This was the scariest thing to go through. No one will truly understand your storm unless they have weathered it as well. This thing is really trying to kill me; my heart percentage dropped, yet again. I just keep getting back up; I refuse to believe this is my time to go; God has too much planned for my life. I know this is not how my story ends.

I can feel my grandmother's wings hugging me, saying, I see you doing work in the church and putting money in the pan, and you are learning some more stories in the bible, even had your name in a few programs, to God be the glory Alston, keep getting back up and doing the right thing.

No prayer is in vain.

Look at the blessings and how you made it through.

Tell the test in your testimony but give

God the praise for the victory.

more than Enough

Make me think of the song He's Done Enough (the version by Fantasia and her mother Diane Barrino)

Scripture

"Cast all your anxiety on Him because He cares for you."
1 Peter 5:7

Prayer... Petitioning Your help

Father God,

I come to you today with a pure heart and as humbly as I know.

Father, I am most grateful for Your word of life. I am thankful for waking up this day.

Father, I'm on bended knee today, petitioning Your help. Father, I need You.

Father, I am a sheep in Your flock, but my wool is black amongst the others.

Father, You said You would wash me white as snow.

Father, I've been abandoned, and I'm lost. Father, You said You would claim me, that You would be my mother and father. Be that to me, O Heavenly Father. Father, I'm last on everyone's list, even my own. Father, You said the last shall be first, and the first shall be last. Father, turn it around. Father, hide me in the midst of the storm. Shine Your presence on me. Father, elevate me higher as I continue to glorify Your name. Forgive all of my sins in Jesus' name. Forgive the hurt and pains of the past. Father, I wish not to remember it or feel it anymore. Father, wipe my tears away and wrap Your arms around me. Hold me tight, and don't let go. I believe You will grant all of these things today in Jesus' name, Amen.

Message... Piecing together

Piecing together instead of picking apart.

When we see others trying to move in a positive direction or trying to do something positive, let's encourage them. Let's cheer them on. Instead of picking it apart, let's help one another pick up the pieces. Most of us are looking for flaws in the way others do things. Can we try pointing them in the right direction or in the direction of someone who can help? Can we try to mentor them? Often, we have to remember when

we first started something. We must remember the support we had or lack thereof. Let's not only be positive for ourselves but for others as well.

Reminder

Unity

Positivity

Spirituality

Appreciation

Remember judge not.

Scripture

"And the God of all grace, who called you to his eternal glory in Christ, after you have suffered a little while, will himself restore you and make you strong, firm and steadfast."

1 Peter 5:10

You can Make It …. Go to the Source

2 Corinthians 12:9 "But he said to me, "My grace is sufficient for you, for my power is made perfect in weakness." Therefore, I will boast all the more gladly about my weaknesses, so that Christ's power may rest on me."

Ephesians 2:8-9 "For it is by grace you have been saved, through faith- and this is not from yourselves, it is the gift of God- ^{9}not by works, so that no one can boast."

Deuteronomy 4:31 "For the LORD your God is a merciful God; he will not abandon or destroy you or forget the covenant with your ancestors, which he confirmed to them by oath."

Ephesians 1:11 "In him we were also chosen, having been predestined according to the plan of him who works out everything in conformity with the purpose of his will."

Psalm 84:11 "For the LORD God is a sun and shield; the LORD bestows favor and honor; no good thing does he withhold from those whose walk is blameless."

Psalm 30:5 "For his anger lasts only a moment, but his favor lasts a lifetime; weeping may stay for the night, but rejoicing comes in the morning."

Though I had my share of storms, we all have and will, just a different name and strength. Everyone may or may not have the convenience of a grandma's house such as mine. It may have been your parents, aunts/uncles, cousins, foster parents, teacher, adoptive parent, a mother/father figure who took care of you and instilled a greater foundation in life for you to do the right thing — to look to the source. It is all to test your faith. You must stand with an unshakeable faith. Though it may hurt, it may leave a hole in your heart and may even leave you devastated. You must have faith that you can and will be restored.

Life has taught me how to pray for the will of God and what He has for me. I learned that I can do all things through Christ. One example, which took me some time to learn, was to pray for a spouse. I knew He had someone for me. I had to go through some things to be ready for the type of person He had for me. Maybe I wasn't ready before; maybe I had to learn a lot more than what I thought I knew. I am so happy now. With everything that I am, I know this was God sent— the love, respect, and loyalty. There is such peace and a sense of calmness in the home.

Everything I went through was well worth it. I'm sharing a life of love, the love that I never thought I would experience. My life is far from perfect, and I am still in a storm, but now I share my dance in the rain, holding hands and smiling. Everything I have prayed for, God has answered. This is what grandma wanted me to learn, who my source is and whom I must lean on. Her words always provided me wisdom and guidance through life's journey, leading me to the Word, more importantly, the Word of God.

Going to God first has proven to me to be most beneficial. If I had listened closely or asked more questions, I could have avoided some mistakes. If I had grasped how to word my prayers, I would have avoided some situations. Look back to some words of wisdom that someone may have told you; it may have been advice given because they've had to learn the hard way. Always look at things with sympathy, empathy, and compassion. We all are a storm away from being in the other person's shoes. Don't be so quick to forget the times you may have been in a similar situation.

Be thankful for all things, the storms in life, the joyous times, the individuals in your life, and the ones that left. Realize that things happen for a reason and that it's not happening to you; it's happening for you. It is just like the cause and effect that you learned in school. The very thing that happened caused you to be in a new and better season. You also must be watchful of the things you pray for. You may pray for a new car, but you might receive one from being in an accident. You may want to say, "Lord, bless me with a car with no harm or danger to anyone." You may be praying that your friend helps with a bill. You proceed to call your friend for it, and they may only have part of what you need. Try praying for unexpected blessings/ unexpected money from unexpected people and places. You just might be unlocking some things that have your name on it that you didn't know. You also should stand on the fact that you can make it. This is just my way of looking at things.

I can't quote a million messages from the bible; I am not a preacher or an evangelist. Not indeed a Sunday school teacher, but I am a child of the Most-High God. A God who lives and covers me every day from the spiritual warfare and attacks of the enemy. I know that the devil has no power over me, and I know I have the victory. God was there in the beginning, He will be there in the middle, and He is waiting for me at the end of any storm. I know I can do anything but fail.

If you are reading this text with tears in your eyes from a storm, you may be experiencing, just know it will soon be over, and you will make it. It may seem as though each storm named in this text is all the storms I had; it's not; there are countless more. It may look like the storms only lasted a few moments; they didn't. This is not to give honor to the storm; this is to give honor to God. It is to let you know you are not alone in life's storm. This is to give you words of wisdom and encouragement. This is to let you know that you, too, can receive the victory. Know that in the beginning, middle, and end of the storm, you must give God praise. Trust God for the answers and the outcome.

You can do it. You can get that job. You can get that raise. You can get that house. You can get that car. You can have that marriage. You can change your lifestyle. You can forgive the individuals who hurt you. You can start over. Claim your season of favor. Your seed has broken ground. It is time for your harvest. Always do the right thing. Always treat people right.

Thinking of a song, it's working (by William Murphy)

The song says, "this is my season of grace and favor. This is my season to reap what I have sown."

Something to remember: No matter the storm, you can get through anything. You must trust God. We cannot avoid life's lessons, but we have to have a good attitude and be thankful for every moment. The storms included. Every second can be your last. Let the small stuff go and be happy. Enjoy your season.

Hurricane Mattie Rose

Out of all the hurricanes, this was the one that I was unable to rebuild from. A storm will cause a hole in your heart, but this one will last forever. So many words were left unspoken because I thought I had time. The time to pray, say the things I always wanted to, and say thank you. When the call came in, it made my heart skip a beat, but there was nothing I could do. I could not fix this one; this was not a lesson that I could make better. I did not see devastation as all the hurricanes before or after when I looked around. All I saw was paradise, memories, and visions of the riches my Father had for them. The beautiful wings they gained and the one-of-a-kind smile they had. Yes, this storm was different. Maybe I was looking at the other storms in the wrong light. I looked at it as if it was taking something away instead of what it brought me. Now, I have them forever; they can never leave me. No state will separate us, neither will a casket, because they can fly with me always — my forever angels.

 I believe every day, especially about my grandmother Rosa (my mother's mother). How she is so proud of me with this book, going to church, and the restored dedication I have for the Lord. That I am finally standing on the foundation, she instilled in me. I know that my grandmother Mattie (my Father's mother) is so delighted that I am on track and never forgot about family.

Message... Time and Regret

So, you assume you have time to be perturbed with someone? You assume you have time to apologize or make it right? We don't know the day nor the hour. God already said that. So, you would willingly live the rest of your life regretting the way you handled a situation or allowing someone else to feel the pain of losing you with unresolved issues? You don't have the book of life to know how much time any of us have. Get it right today. If you've tried, keep on trying and keep on praying—right the wrongs of yesterday and today. Release the dead weight.

Message...Unexpected

Be an unexpected blessing to someone today, whether it's a positive phone call, a healthy conversation, or an encouraging word. It just might be the thing they need. It can easily be simple, like a smile and/or the joy of laughter that gets a person over the hump. Think about the time you hoped the phone would ring to brighten your day. Let's spread positivity and love to the unexpected today.

Amen.

Summary

Prayers and Wisdom from Grandma's House

Inspirational Warmth and Guidance through Life's Journey

Life will produce enough highs and lows. Alston Shropshire's will be no different. You, likewise, may have had your share of these journeys. Alston is becoming weaker because of life's discord, confusion, and endless disappointments. A propelling force and a miraculous measure of vitality will produce change with perseverance and resilience. A life-shifting illness will cause an absolute test. Alston will have to look deeply at the word faith.

Sounds familiar? Have you experienced a breaking point, a life-shifting event, day-to-day challenges, loss of a job? What about the death of a parent, child, or loved one? How about bullying, debt, bankruptcy, divorce, illness, or countless others? Thus, you, too, have had your FAITH tested. Countless trials and tribulations throughout half of a lifetime will at least have you at the point where you are guessing, "How will I get through this?"

Alston goes back to the introduction of the countless prayer and words of wisdom of a calm voice and spirit, Grandma. The matriarch of the family. The one who prayed and fasted and attended church. No one had a stronger influence.

In this text, you will view the exceptional wisdom and prayers that she shared with Alston. These were the things shared daily. Prayers and good conversations will be necessary for life ahead. Alston did not comprehend just how firm standing on the Rock would be and how the presence of grandma's house, with those prayers and wisdom sayings, would revive and propel a commitment to the Lord and exercise His Word.

Alston Shropshire is a first-time author, stepping out on faith to distribute inspirational prayers and words of wisdom with people. The most important attributes learned from grandma's house. Alston craves to strengthen others. Alston wants to share the events that were so essential in bleak moments, and joyful celebrations took a leap of faith and focused on those subjects showed in Grandma's house.

www.ingramcontent.com/pod-product-compliance
Lightning Source LLC
Chambersburg PA
CBHW060044230426
43661CB00004B/645